This Book Belongs To:

_____

- For more free activity sheets visit: Learninreturn.com

AMERICAN WHITE PELICAN

Notes:

Where it was found?

Time it was found?

Animal Identification:
(Approximate size,
young or adult, color
or any unique marks)

How many are there?

What is it doing?

PHOTO OR ROUGH SKETCH OF ANIMAL

BADGER

☐ Notes:

Where it was found?

Time it was found?

Animal Identification:
(Approximate size,
young or adult, color
or any unique marks)

How many are there?

What is it doing?

PHOTO OR ROUGH SKETCH OF ANIMAL

BALD EAGLE

☐ Notes:

Where it was found?

Time it was found?

Animal Identification:
(Approximate size,
young or adult, color
or any unique marks)

How many are there?

What is it doing?

PHOTO OR ROUGH SKETCH OF ANIMAL

BAT

Notes:

Where it was found?

Time it was found?

Animal Identification:
(Approximate size,
young or adult, color
or any unique marks)

How many are there?

What is it doing?

PHOTO OR ROUGH SKETCH OF ANIMAL

BEAVER

☐ Notes:

Where it was found?

Time it was found?

Animal Identification:
(Approximate size,
young or adult, color
or any unique marks)

How many are there?

What is it doing?

PHOTO OR ROUGH SKETCH OF ANIMAL

BADGER

Notes:

Where it was found?

Time it was found?

Animal Identification:
(Approximate size,
young or adult, color
or any unique marks)

How many are there?

What is it doing?

PHOTO OR ROUGH SKETCH OF ANIMAL

BISON

☐ Notes:

Where it was found?

Time it was found?

Animal Identification:
(Approximate size,
young or adult, color
or any unique marks)

How many are there?

What is it doing?

PHOTO OR ROUGH SKETCH OF ANIMAL

BIG HORN SHEEP

☐ Notes:

Where it was found?

Time it was found?

Animal Identification:
(Approximate size,
young or adult, color
or any unique marks)

How many are there?

What is it doing?

PHOTO OR ROUGH SKETCH OF ANIMAL

BLACK BEAR

Notes:

Where it was found?

Time it was found?

Animal Identification:
(Approximate size,
young or adult, color
or any unique marks)

How many are there?

What is it doing?

PHOTO OR ROUGH SKETCH OF ANIMAL

BOBCAT

☐

Notes:

Where it was found?

Time it was found?

Animal Identification:
(Approximate size,
young or adult, color
or any unique marks)

How many are there?

What is it doing?

PHOTO OR ROUGH SKETCH OF ANIMAL

CANADA GOOSE

☐ Notes:

Where it was found?

Time it was found?

Animal Identification:
(Approximate size,
young or adult, color
or any unique marks)

How many are there?

What is it doing?

PHOTO OR ROUGH SKETCH OF ANIMAL

CANADA LYNX

☐ Notes:

Where it was found?

Time it was found?

Animal Identification:
(Approximate size,
young or adult, color
or any unique marks)

How many are there?

What is it doing?

PHOTO OR ROUGH SKETCH OF ANIMAL

CHIPMUNK

☐ Notes:

Where it was found?

Time it was found?

Animal Identification:
(Approximate size,
young or adult, color
or any unique marks)

How many are there?

What is it doing?

PHOTO OR ROUGH SKETCH OF ANIMAL

COUGAR

☐ Notes:

Where it was found?

Time it was found?

Animal Identification:
(Approximate size,
young or adult, color
or any unique marks)

How many are there?

What is it doing?

PHOTO OR ROUGH SKETCH OF ANIMAL

COYOTE

Notes:

Where it was found?

Time it was found?

Animal Identification:
(Approximate size,
young or adult, color
or any unique marks)

How many are there?

What is it doing?

PHOTO OR ROUGH SKETCH OF ANIMAL

ELK

Notes:

Where it was found?

Time it was found?

Animal Identification:
(Approximate size,
young or adult, color
or any unique marks)

How many are there?

What is it doing?

PHOTO OR ROUGH SKETCH OF ANIMAL

GOLDEN EAGLE

☐ Notes:

Where it was found?

Time it was found?

Animal Identification:
(Approximate size,
young or adult, color
or any unique marks)

How many are there?

What is it doing?

PHOTO OR ROUGH SKETCH OF ANIMAL

GOLDEN MANTLED GROUND SQUIRREL

☐

Notes:

Where it was found?

Time it was found?

Animal Identification:
(Approximate size,
young or adult, color
or any unique marks)

How many are there?

What is it doing?

PHOTO OR ROUGH SKETCH OF ANIMAL

GRAY WOLF

Notes:

Where it was found?

Time it was found?

Animal Identification:
(Approximate size,
young or adult, color
or any unique marks)

How many are there?

What is it doing?

PHOTO OR ROUGH SKETCH OF ANIMAL

GREAT HORNED OWL

Notes:

Where it was found?

Time it was found?

Animal Identification:
(Approximate size,
young or adult, color
or any unique marks)

How many are there?

What is it doing?

PHOTO OR ROUGH SKETCH OF ANIMAL

GRIZZLY BEAR

☐ Notes:

Where it was found?

Time it was found?

Animal Identification:
(Approximate size,
young or adult, color
or any unique marks)

How many are there?

What is it doing?

PHOTO OR ROUGH SKETCH OF ANIMAL

MALLARD

☐ Notes:

Where it was found?

Time it was found?

Animal Identification:
(Approximate size,
young or adult, color
or any unique marks)

How many are there?

What is it doing?

PHOTO OR ROUGH SKETCH OF ANIMAL

MARMOT

☐ Notes:

Where it was found?

Time it was found?

Animal Identification:
(Approximate size,
young or adult, color
or any unique marks)

How many are there?

What is it doing?

PHOTO OR ROUGH SKETCH OF ANIMAL

MARTEN

Notes:

Where it was found?

Time it was found?

Animal Identification:
(Approximate size,
young or adult, color
or any unique marks)

How many are there?

What is it doing?

PHOTO OR ROUGH SKETCH OF ANIMAL

MOOSE

☐ Notes:

Where it was found?

Time it was found?

Animal Identification:
(Approximate size,
young or adult, color
or any unique marks)

How many are there?

What is it doing?

PHOTO OR ROUGH SKETCH OF ANIMAL

MOUNTAIN GOAT

☐

Notes:

Where it was found?

Time it was found?

Animal Identification:
(Approximate size,
young or adult, color
or any unique marks)

How many are there?

What is it doing?

PHOTO OR ROUGH SKETCH OF ANIMAL

MULE DEER

☐ Notes:

Where it was found?

Time it was found?

Animal Identification:
(Approximate size,
young or adult, color
or any unique marks)

How many are there?

What is it doing?

PHOTO OR ROUGH SKETCH OF ANIMAL

OSPREY

Notes:

Where it was found?

Time it was found?

Animal Identification:
(Approximate size,
young or adult, color
or any unique marks)

How many are there?

What is it doing?

PHOTO OR ROUGH SKETCH OF ANIMAL

PEREGRINE FALCON

☐ Notes:

Where it was found? | Time it was found?

Animal Identification:
(Approximate size,
young or adult, color
or any unique marks)

How many are there?

What is it doing?

PHOTO OR ROUGH SKETCH OF ANIMAL

PIKA

Notes:

Where it was found?

Time it was found?

Animal Identification:
(Approximate size,
young or adult, color
or any unique marks)

How many are there?

What is it doing?

PHOTO OR ROUGH SKETCH OF ANIMAL

PRONGHORN

 ☐ Notes:

Where it was found?

Time it was found?

Animal Identification:
(Approximate size,
young or adult, color
or any unique marks)

How many are there?

What is it doing?

PHOTO OR ROUGH SKETCH OF ANIMAL

RAVEN

☐ Notes:

| Where it was found? | Time it was found? |

Animal Identification:
(Approximate size,
young or adult, color
or any unique marks)

How many are there?

What is it doing?

PHOTO OR ROUGH SKETCH OF ANIMAL

RED FOX

☐ Notes:

Where it was found?

Time it was found?

Animal Identification:
(Approximate size,
young or adult, color
or any unique marks)

How many are there?

What is it doing?

PHOTO OR ROUGH SKETCH OF ANIMAL

RED SQUIRREL

☐ Notes:

Where it was found?

Time it was found?

Animal Identification:
(Approximate size,
young or adult, color
or any unique marks)

How many are there?

What is it doing?

PHOTO OR ROUGH SKETCH OF ANIMAL

RED TAILED HAWK

Notes:

Where it was found?

Time it was found?

Animal Identification:
(Approximate size,
young or adult, color
or any unique marks)

How many are there?

What is it doing?

PHOTO OR ROUGH SKETCH OF ANIMAL

RIVER OTTER

☐

Notes:

Where it was found?

Time it was found?

Animal Identification:
(Approximate size,
young or adult, color
or any unique marks)

How many are there?

What is it doing?

PHOTO OR ROUGH SKETCH OF ANIMAL

SANDHILL CRANE

☐ Notes:

Where it was found?

Time it was found?

Animal Identification:
(Approximate size,
young or adult, color
or any unique marks)

How many are there?

What is it doing?

PHOTO OR ROUGH SKETCH OF ANIMAL

SNOWSHOE HARE

Notes:

Where it was found?

Time it was found?

Animal Identification:
(Approximate size,
young or adult, color
or any unique marks)

How many are there?

What is it doing?

PHOTO OR ROUGH SKETCH OF ANIMAL

TIGER SALAMANDER

Notes:

Where it was found?

Time it was found?

Animal Identification:
(Approximate size,
young or adult, color
or any unique marks)

How many are there?

What is it doing?

PHOTO OR ROUGH SKETCH OF ANIMAL

WHITE TAILED DEER

☐ Notes:

Where it was found?

Time it was found?

Animal Identification:
(Approximate size,
young or adult, color
or any unique marks)

How many are there?

What is it doing?

PHOTO OR ROUGH SKETCH OF ANIMAL

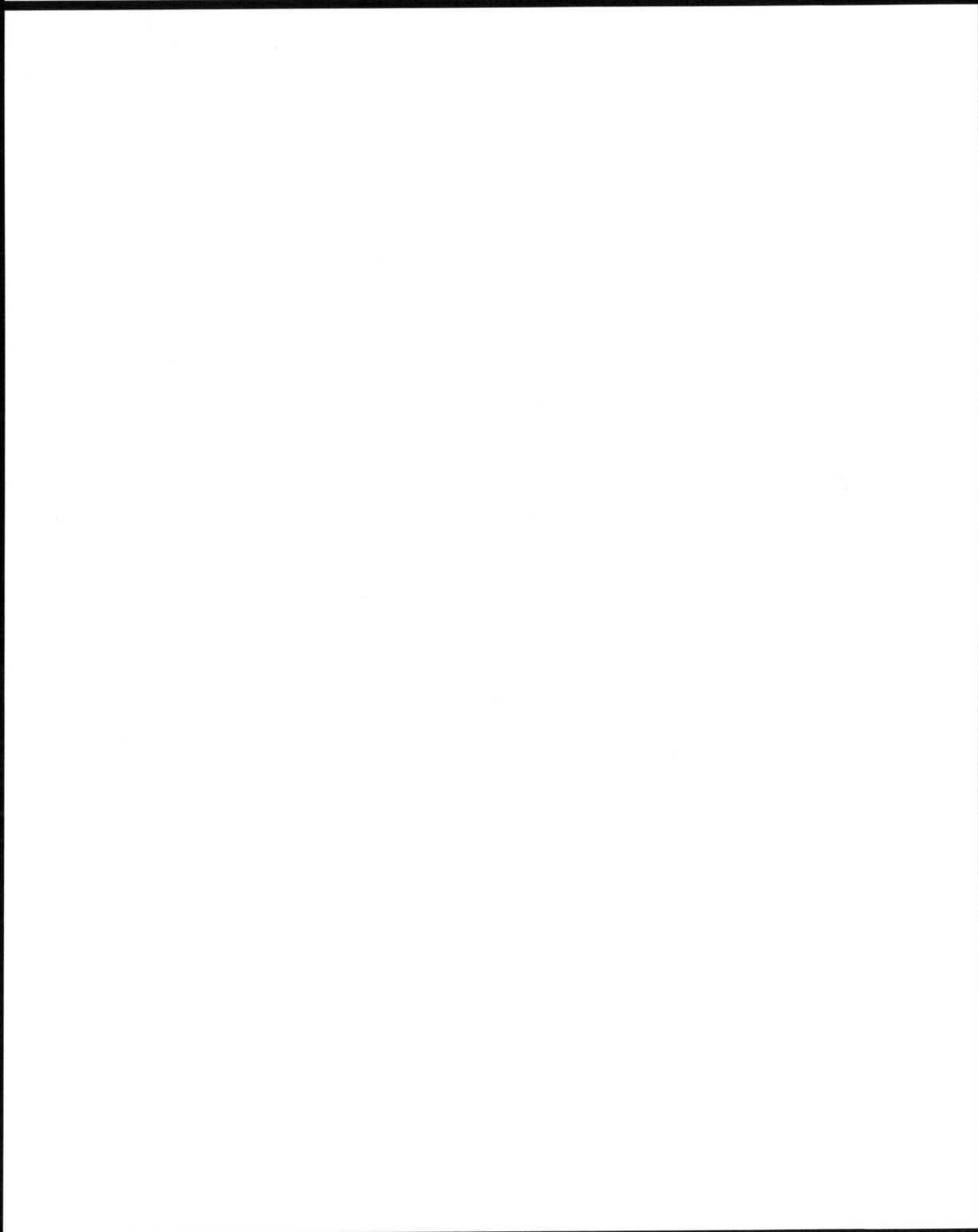

WHITE TAILED JACK RABBIT

Notes:

Where it was found?

Time it was found?

Animal Identification:
(Approximate size,
young or adult, color
or any unique marks)

How many are there?

What is it doing?

PHOTO OR ROUGH SKETCH OF ANIMAL

WOLVERINE

☐ Notes:

Where it was found?

Time it was found?

Animal Identification:
(Approximate size,
young or adult, color
or any unique marks)

How many are there?

What is it doing?

PHOTO OR ROUGH SKETCH OF ANIMAL

UINTA GROUND SQUIRREL

Notes:

Where it was found?

Time it was found?

Animal Identification:
(Approximate size,
young or adult, color
or any unique marks)

How many are there?

What is it doing?

PHOTO OR ROUGH SKETCH OF ANIMAL

Made in the USA
Middletown, DE
09 June 2025